Harry Potter™

A STICKER COLLECTION

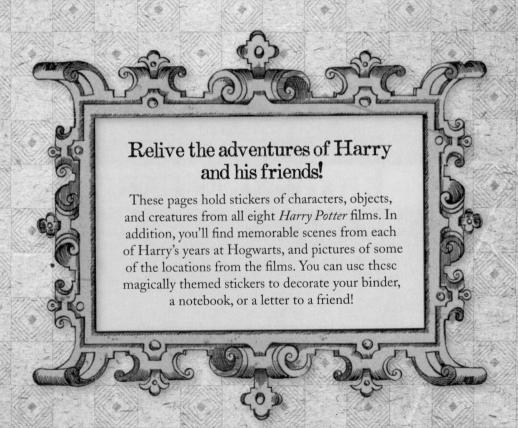

Relive the adventures of Harry and his friends!

These pages hold stickers of characters, objects, and creatures from all eight *Harry Potter* films. In addition, you'll find memorable scenes from each of Harry's years at Hogwarts, and pictures of some of the locations from the films. You can use these magically themed stickers to decorate your binder, a notebook, or a letter to a friend!

WIZARDING WORLD

INSIGHT EDITIONS
San Rafael, California

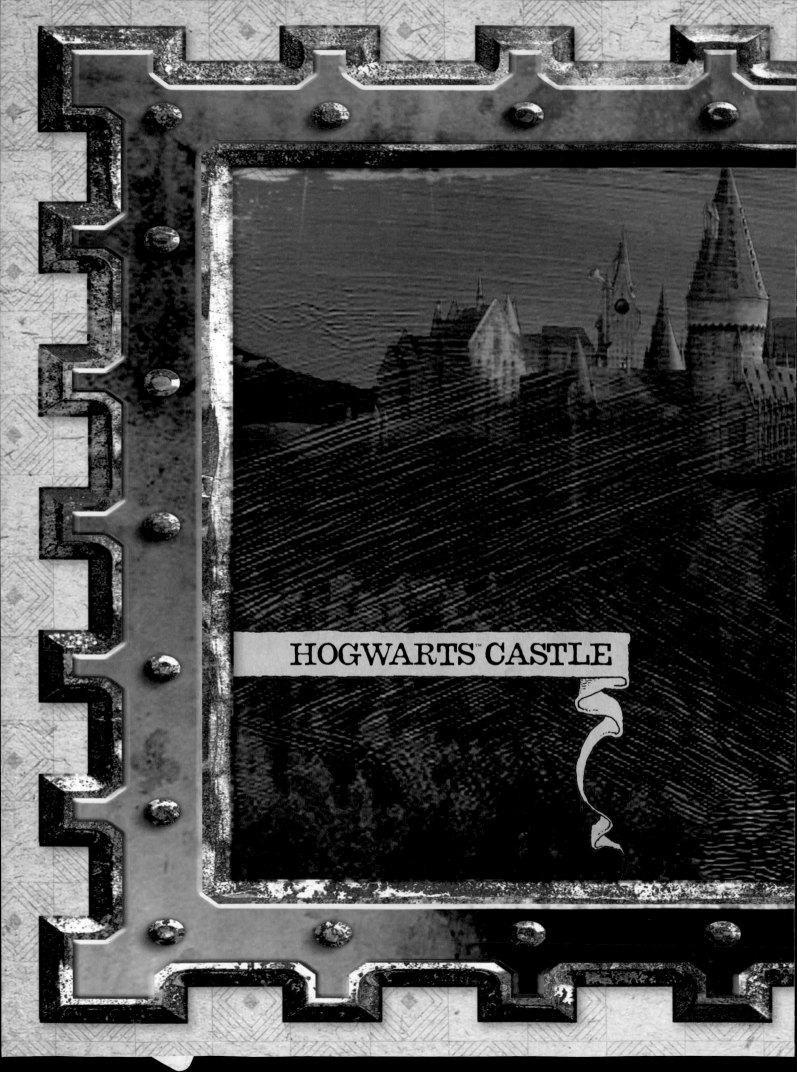

HOGWARTS™ CASTLE

HARRY POTTER™

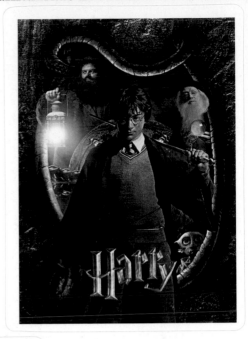

UNDESIRABLE №1

HARRY POTTER

CONTACT THE MINISTRY OF MAGIC IMMEDIATELY IF YOU HAVE ANY INFORMATION CONCERNING HIS WHEREABOUTS. FAILING TO REPORT WILL RESULT IN IMPRISONMENT.

REWARD 10,000 GALLEONS ON HIS HEAD

Harry

Gryffindor
C
Captain ™

HERMIONE GRANGER™

HERMIONE GRANGER™

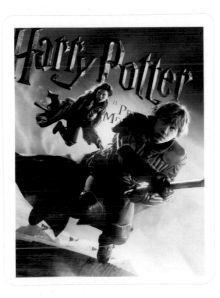

MAGICAL BEASTS, CREATURES, AND BEINGS

Hungarian Horntail

Buckbeak

Nagini

Aragog

Thestrals

Merperson

Werewolf

Fawkes

MAGICAL BEASTS, CREATURES, AND BEINGS

Monster Book of Monsters

Owl

Norbert

Dobby

Cornish Pixie

Fluffy

Grindylow

Centaurs

Dementors

HOGWARTS STAFF

Professor
Flitwick

Professor
Trelawney

Professor
Dumbledore™

Professor
McGonagall

Rubeus Hagrid™

Professor
Umbridge

Argus
Filch

Professor
Slughorn

Professor
Snape

™ & © WBIE (s11)

ORDER OF THE PHOENIX™

Mad-Eye Moody

Remus Lupin

Sirius Black

Arthur Weasley

Albus Dumbledore

Kingsley Shacklebolt

Tonks

Hagrid

ORDER
OF THE PHOENIX

Molly Weasley

ORDER
OF THE PHOENIX

VOLDEMORT™ AND THE DEATH EATERS

Lord Voldemort™

Death Eater Masks

Bellatrix Lestrange

Wormtail

VOLDEMORT™ AND THE DEATH EATERS

Lord Voldemort™

Fenrir Greyback

Lucius Malfoy

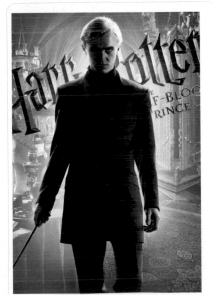

Draco Malfoy™

HOGWARTS HOUSES

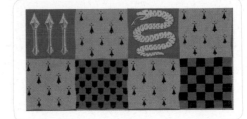

GRYFFINDOR

SLYTHERIN

The Fat Lady

HUFFLEPUFF

RAVENCLAW

™ & © WBIE (s11)

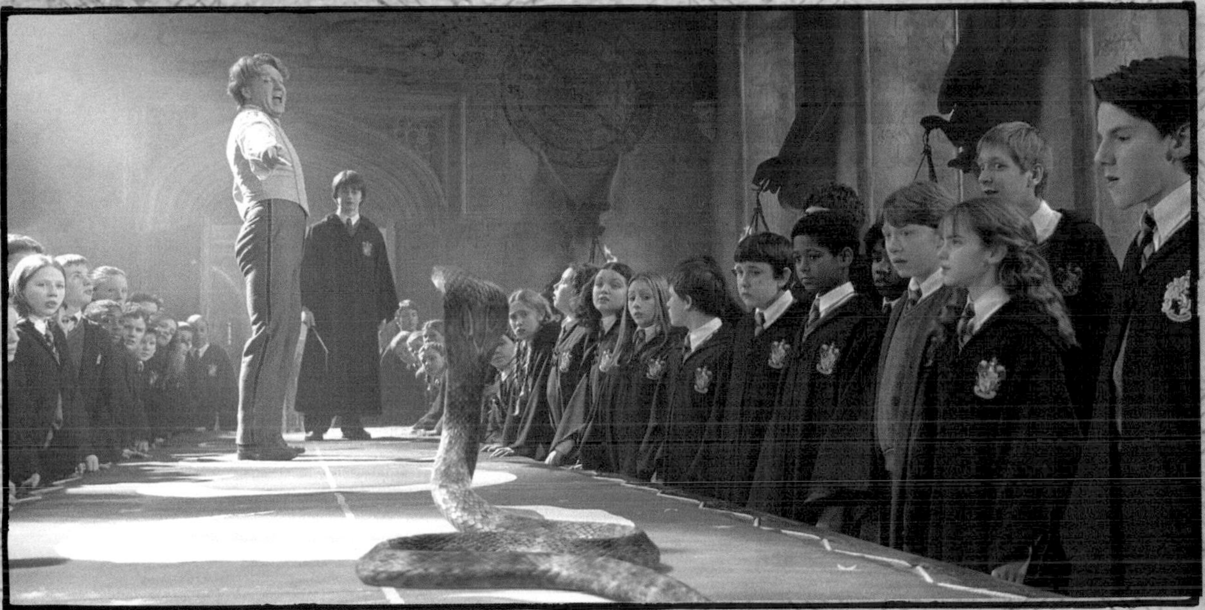

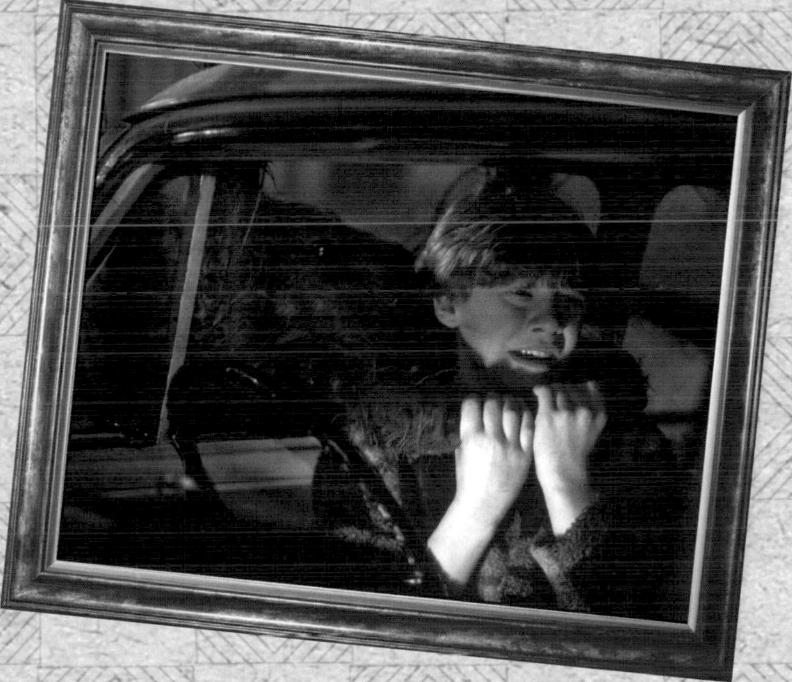

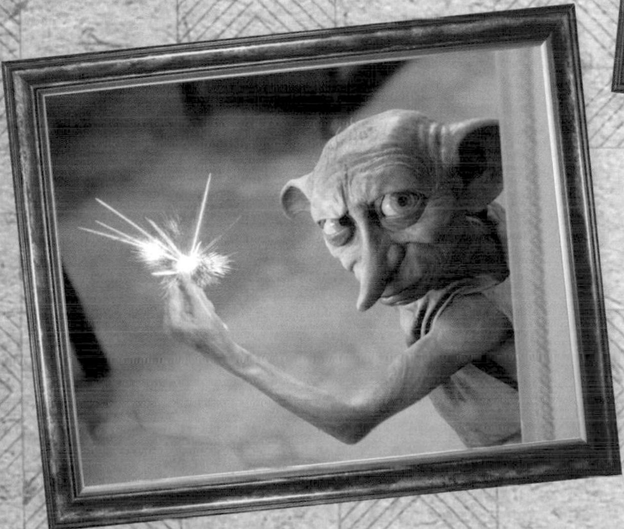

HOGSMEADE

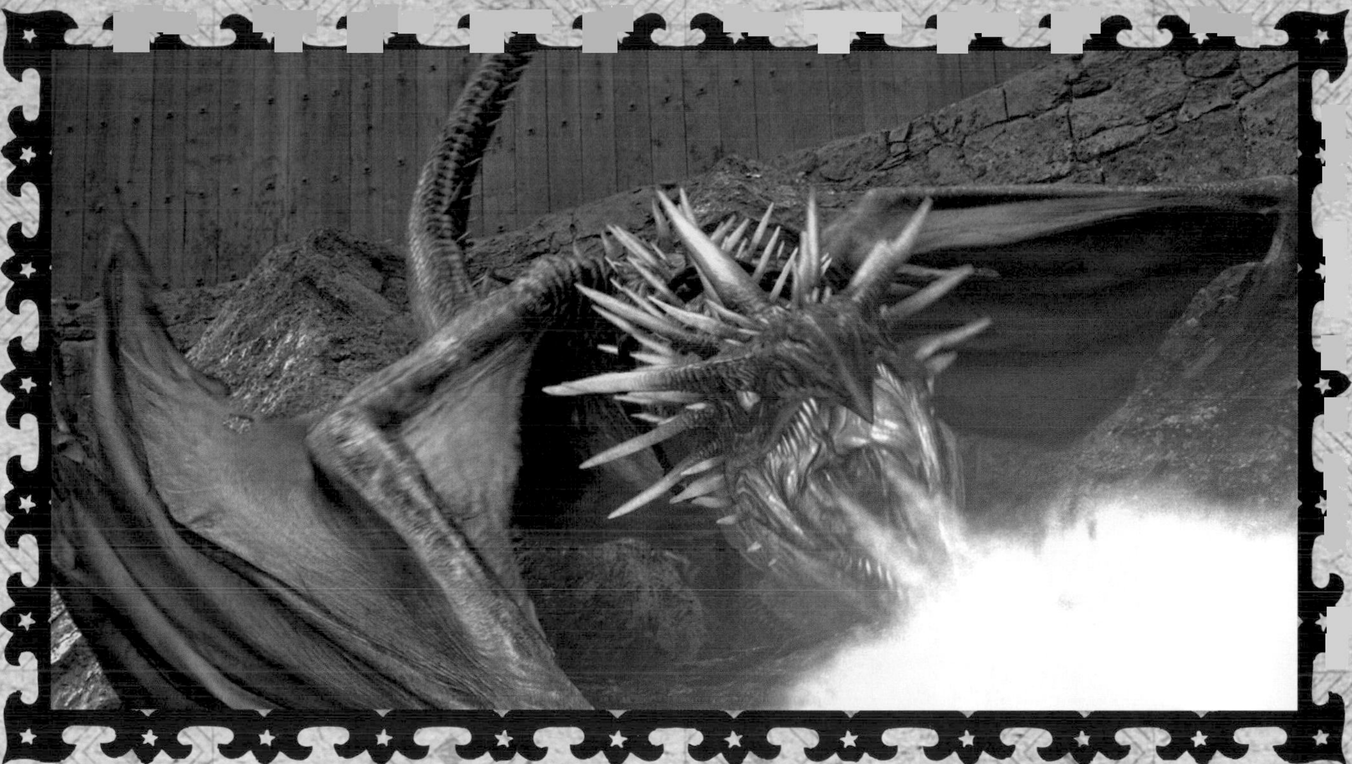

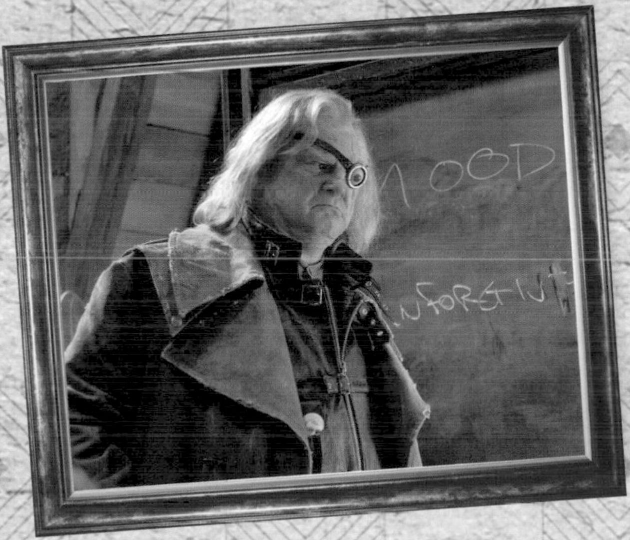

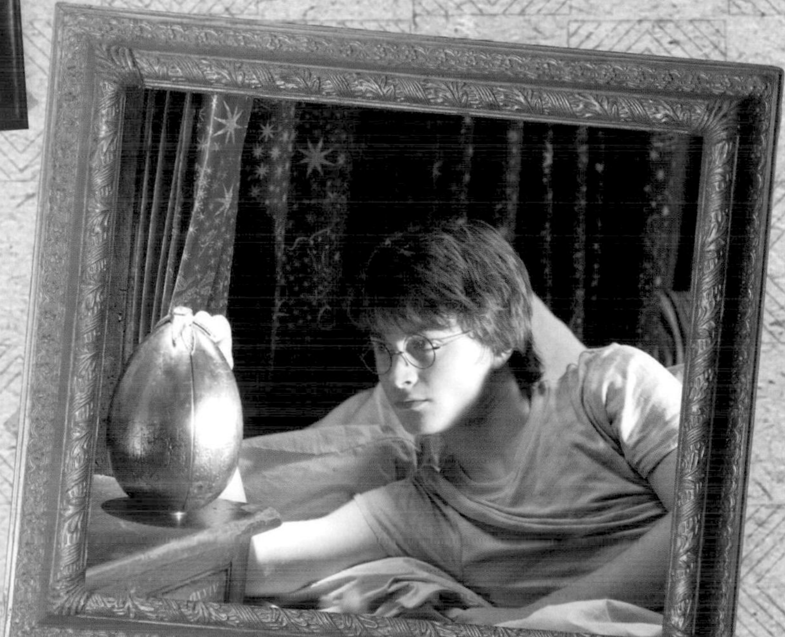

THE ATRIUM AT THE MINISTRY OF MAGIC

DUMBLEDORE'S ARMY

Harry Potter™

Ginny Weasley™

Neville Longbottom™

Hermione Granger™

Ron Weasley™

Luna Lovegood™

Seamus Finnegan, Neville Longbottom,
and Dean Thomas

Fred, Ron, Ginny, and George Weasley

Cho Chang

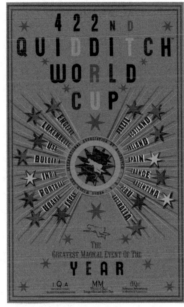

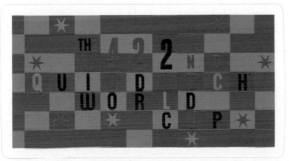

POTIONS

LACEWING FLIES
A 0752
FROM THE APOTHECARIUM OF HORACE E. F. SLUGHORN

POLYJUICE POTION
A 0052
FROM THE APOTHECARIUM OF HORACE E. F. SLUGHORN

BOOMSLANG SKIN
A 0002
FROM THE APOTHECARIUM OF HORACE E. F. SLUGHORN

SLEEPING DRAUGHT
A 0075
FROM THE APOTHECARIUM OF HORACE E. F. SLUGHORN

☠ **PORCUPINE PARTS** ☠
L. 50
FROM THE APOTHECARIUM OF HORACE E. F. SLUGHORN

MANDRAKE ELIXIR
39423
FROM THE APOTHECARIUM OF HORACE E. F. SLUGHORN

No. Bezoars
E. M. L. POTIONS CO.

EXTREMELY POISONOUS
POTION N.86
CONTAINS: POWDERED MOONSTONE & SYRUP OF HELLEBORE
№ 65487
L. 150

FROM THE APOTHECARIUM OF
HORACE E. F. SLUGHORN
CC 61042

EXTREMELY POISONOUS
POTION N.07
CONTAINS: ESSENCE OF VENOMOUS TENTACULA & POWDERED LIONFISH
№ 66548
L. 150

EXTREMELY POISONOUS
POTION N.113
CONTAINS: JOBBERKNOLL FEATHERS & SYRUP OF ARNICA
№ 48765
L. 151

LIBATIUS BORAGE'S
ADVANCED POTION-MAKING

MAGICAL TRANSPORTATION

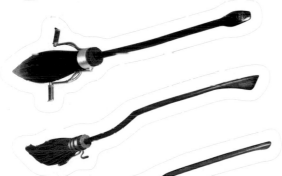

MAGICAL ITEMS

Sorting Hat

Boggart
Jack-in-the
Box

Time-Turner

Golden Egg

Golden Snitch

Quick-Quotes Quill

Mirror of
Erised

MAGICAL ITEMS

The Deathly Hallows

The Deathly Hallows

Sword of Gryffindor

Marauder's Map

Elder Wand

Vanishing Cabinet

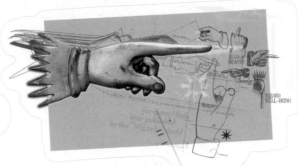

WEASLEYS' WIZARD WHEEZES

WEASLEYS' WIZARD WHEEZES

JUMPING
SNAKES

GHASTLY GARROTING GRASS SNAKES

JOKE WANDS

WEASLEY MEGA BOX

JINX -OFF

KIT INCLUDES CLOAK, HAT & GLOVES

MADE IN ENGLAND

COMPENDIUM BOX OF PYROTECHTRIX

SCREAMING

SCREAMING YO-YO

SCREAMING

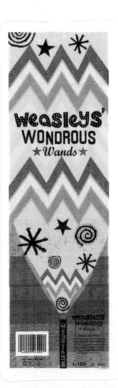

Weasleys' WONDROUS
★Wands★

JUST LIKE THAT HAT

WEASLEY &

WEASLEYS' FAMOUS
UNLUCKY DIP!

BOX O' ROCKETS

TRIWIZARD TOURNAMENT

Cedric Diggory

Viktor Krum

Fleur Delacour

Harry Potter™

THE YULE BALL

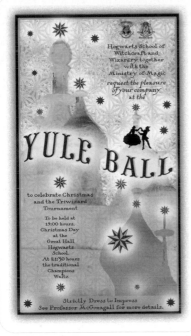

Viktor Krum, Fleur Delacour, and Cedric Diggory

Ginny Weasley

Harry Potter™

The Patil twins with Harry and Ron

Ron
Weasley™

Victor Krum and Hermione Granger™

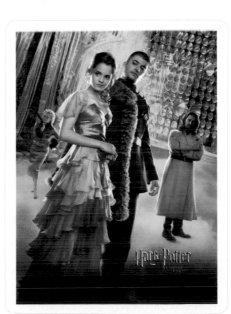

THE MINISTRY OF MAGIC

WANTED
FENRIR GREYBACK

FENRIR GREYBACK IS A SAVAGE WEREWOLF.
CONVICTED MURDERER. SUSPECTED DEATH EATER.

★ APPROACH WITH EXTREME CAUTION! ★

IF YOU HAVE ANY INFORMATION CONCERNING
THIS PERSON, PLEASE CONTACT YOUR
NEAREST AUROR OFFICE.

★ REWARD ★

MINISTRY OF MAGIC

CAUGHT
LUCIUS MALFOY

CONSTANT VIGILANCE!

DEATH EATERS ARE AMONG US!

★ REMEMBER: NEGLIGENCE COSTS LIVES ★

IF YOU HAVE ANY INFORMATION CONCERNING
DEATH EATERS, PLEASE CONTACT YOUR
NEAREST AUROR OFFICE.

★ REWARD ★

HAVE YOU SEEN THIS WIZARD?

AZKABAN PRISON

APPROACH WITH EXTREME CAUTION!
DO NOT ATTEMPT TO USE
MAGIC AGAINST THIS MAN

Any information leading to the arrest of this
man shall be duly rewarded
Notify immediately by owl the Ministry of Magic

DEPARTMENT OF MAGICAL
DM AC
ACCIDENTS AND CATASTROPHES

WANTED
BELLATRIX LESTRANGE

BELLATRIX LESTRANGE IS A KNOWN DEATH EATER.
CONVICTED MURDERER. FUGITIVE FROM AZKABAN.

★ APPROACH WITH EXTREME CAUTION! ★

IF YOU HAVE ANY INFORMATION CONCERNING
THIS PERSON, PLEASE CONTACT YOUR
NEAREST AUROR OFFICE.

★ REWARD ★

DM LE
DEPARTMENT OF
MAGICAL LAW ENFORCEMENT

DEPT. OF
MICo
INTERNATIONAL
MAGICAL CO-OPERATION

500 GALLEONS ON ANY INFORMATION REGARDING DEATH EATERS
SEE INSIDE FOR FULL DETAILS PG. 3

TM & © WBIE (s11)

WEASLEYS' WIZARD WHEEZES IN DIAGON ALLEY